NATIONAL
GEOGRAPHIC
KiDS

weird
but
true!

HUMAN BODY

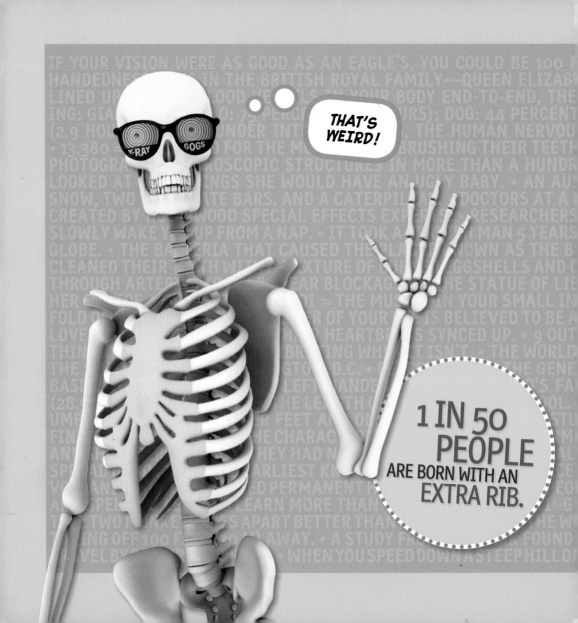

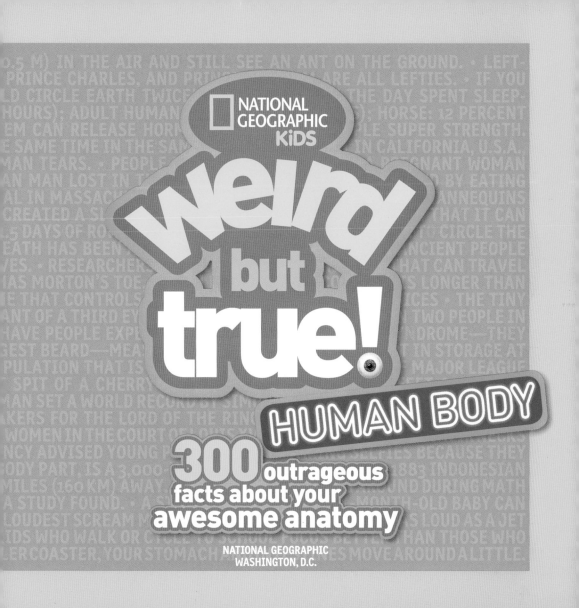

NATIONAL GEOGRAPHIC KiDS

weird but true!

HUMAN BODY

300 outrageous facts about your awesome anatomy

NATIONAL GEOGRAPHIC
WASHINGTON, D.C.

THERE ARE ABOUT

600 hairs

IN A HUMAN

eyebrow.

4

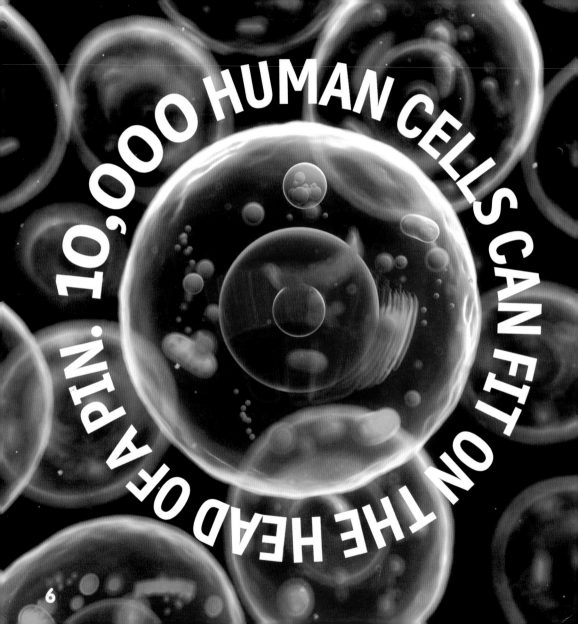

10,000 HUMAN CELLS CAN FIT ON THE HEAD OF A PIN.

6

YOUR STOMACH IS SHAPED LIKE THE LETTER J.

7 IN 10 AMERICAN WOMEN DYE THEIR HAIR.

IN ROMANIA AND TURKEY, YOU CAN'T GET A DRIVER'S LICENSE IF YOU'RE COLOR-BLIND.

AMERICAN ADULTS SPEND ABOUT TWO AND A HALF HOURS A DAY EATING OR DRINKING.

An onion has more DNA than a human does.

HETEROCHROMIA=
WHEN PEOPLE HAVE TWO DIFFERENT-COLORED EYES

In Japan, the movie *Inside Out* was called *Inside Head*.

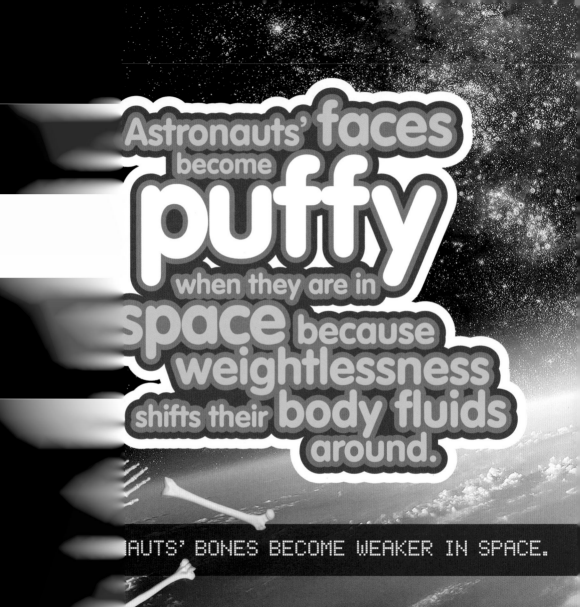

Astronauts' **faces** become **puffy** when they are in **space** because **weightlessness** shifts their **body fluids** around.

AUTS' BONES BECOME WEAKER IN SPACE.

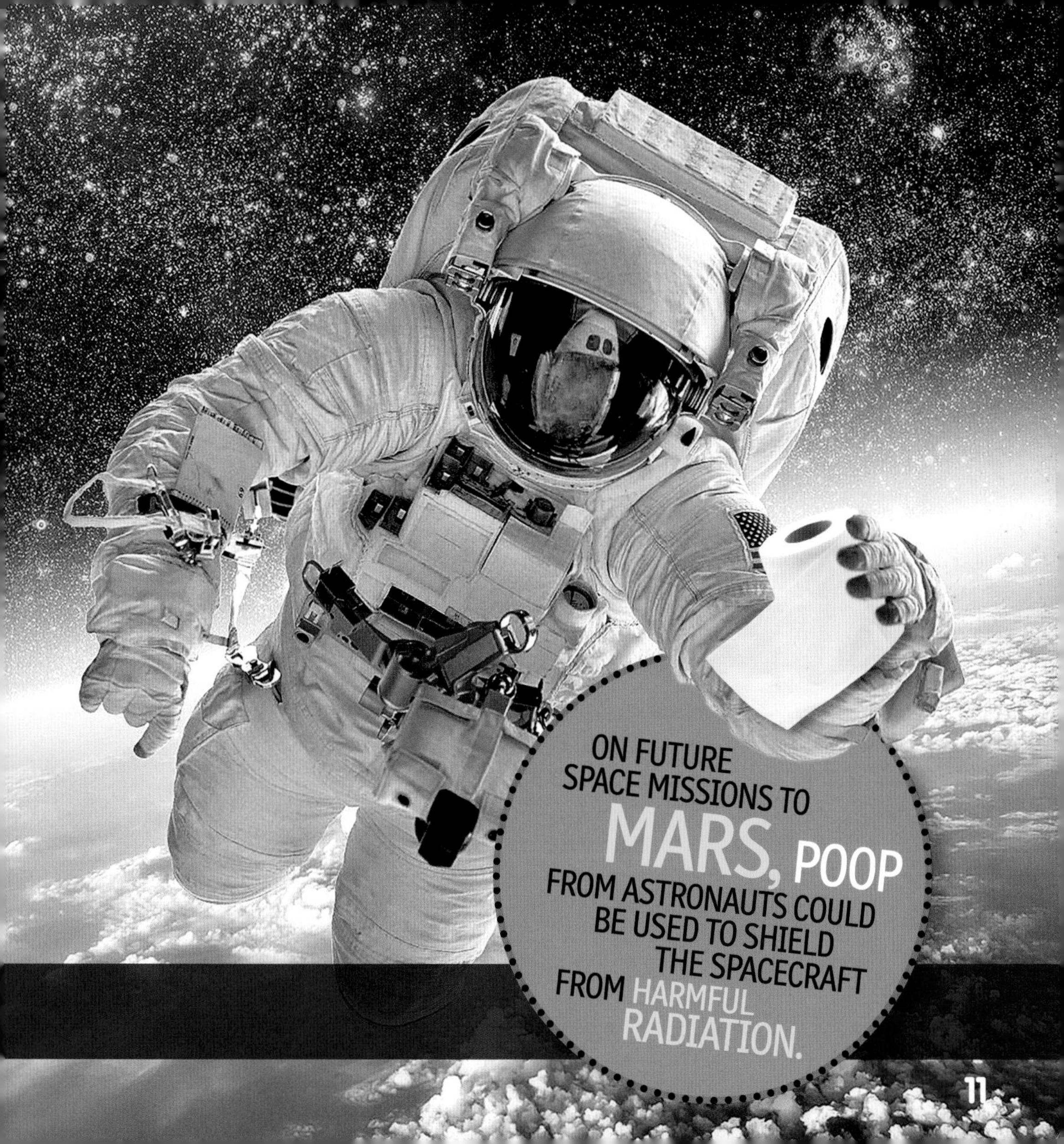

ON FUTURE
SPACE MISSIONS TO
MARS, POOP
FROM ASTRONAUTS COULD
BE USED TO SHIELD
THE SPACECRAFT
FROM HARMFUL
RADIATION.

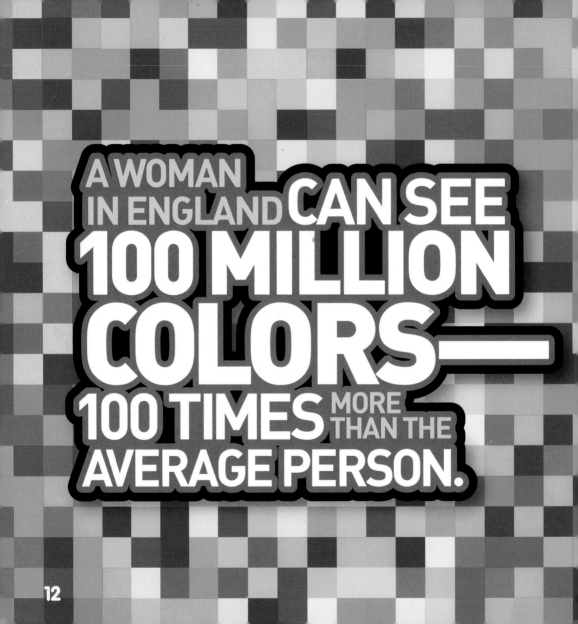

A WOMAN IN ENGLAND CAN SEE 100 MILLION COLORS— 100 TIMES MORE THAN THE AVERAGE PERSON.

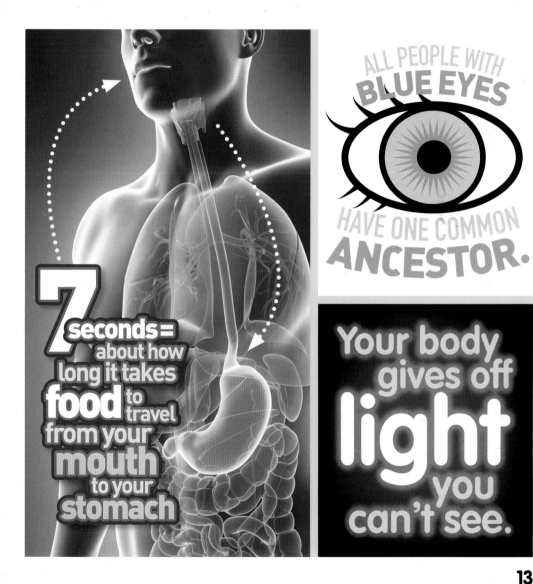

7 seconds = about how long it takes **food** to travel from your **mouth** to your **stomach**

ALL PEOPLE WITH **BLUE EYES** HAVE ONE COMMON **ANCESTOR.**

Your body gives off **light** you can't see.

+1,000

YOUR PUPILS GET BIGGER WHEN YOUR MATH PROBLEMS GET HARDER.

THE **LIVER** IS THE ONLY ORGAN THAT CAN GROW BACK IF PART OF IT IS REMOVED.

IF YOUR **VISION** WERE AS GOOD AS AN **EAGLE'S,** YOU COULD BE **100 FEET** (30.5 m) IN **AIR** THE **AND STILL SEE AN ANT ON THE GROUND.**

EATING DARK CHOCOLATE MAY IMPROVE YOUR ATTENTION SPAN.

LEFT-HANDEDNESS RUNS IN THE BRITISH ROYAL FAMILY— QUEEN ELIZABETH II, PRINCE CHARLES, AND PRINCE WILLIAM ARE ALL LEFTIES.

A **kid** IS MORE LIKELY TO BREAK A **wrist** THAN ANY OTHER **BONE** IN THE **body.**

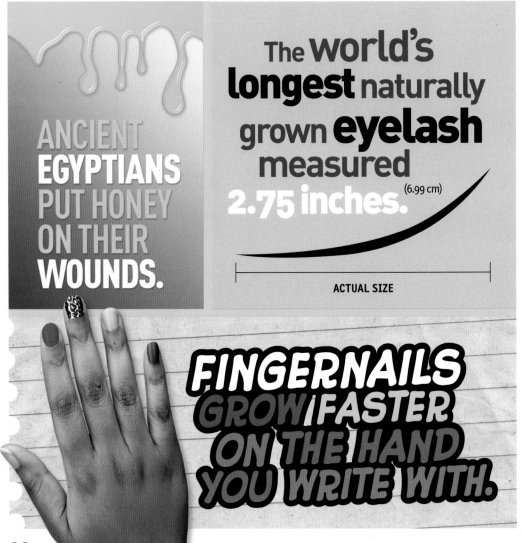

ANCIENT
EGYPTIANS
PUT HONEY
ON THEIR
WOUNDS.

The **world's** **longest** naturally grown **eyelash** measured **2.75 inches.** (6.99 cm)

ACTUAL SIZE

FINGERNAILS GROW FASTER ON THE HAND YOU WRITE WITH.

If you lined up all the **blood vessels** in your body end to end, they would circle Earth twice!

MOST OF YOUR

EAR IS ACTUALLY

INSIDE YOUR

HEAD.

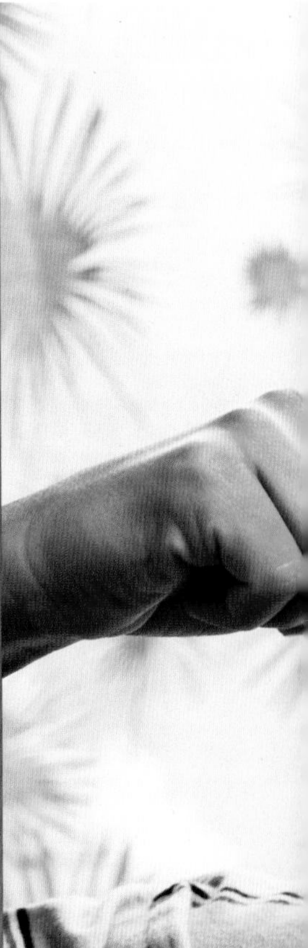

YOUR **EARDRUMS** DON'T **SWEAT.**

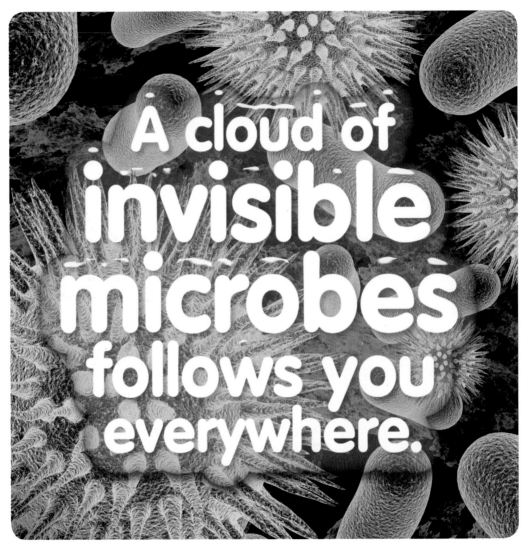

A cloud of invisible microbes follows you everywhere.

HUMAN HAIR HAS BEEN USED TO CLEAN UP OIL SPILLS.

IN JAPAN, IT IS WIDELY BELIEVED THAT A PERSON'S BLOOD TYPE INFLUENCES THEIR PERSONALITY.

An adult's TONGUE is about as long as a SLICE of American cheese.

SWEATING CAN HELP PREVENT COLDS.

25

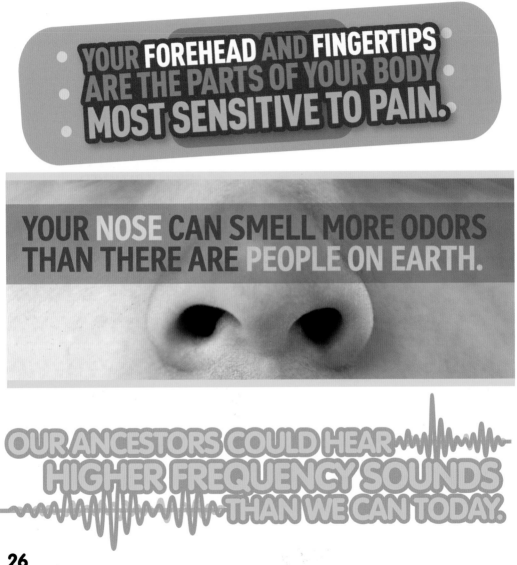

YOUR **FOREHEAD** AND **FINGERTIPS** ARE THE PARTS OF YOUR BODY MOST SENSITIVE TO PAIN.

YOUR **NOSE** CAN SMELL MORE ODORS THAN THERE ARE **PEOPLE ON EARTH.**

OUR ANCESTORS COULD HEAR HIGHER FREQUENCY SOUNDS THAN WE CAN TODAY.

26

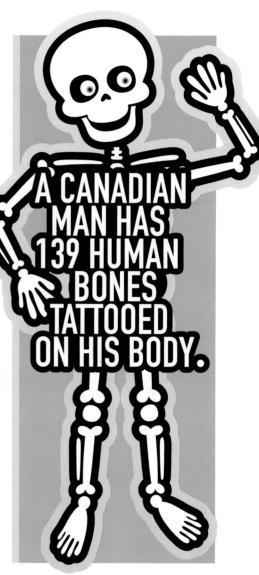

A CANADIAN MAN HAS 139 HUMAN BONES TATTOOED ON HIS BODY.

There's less blood in your body than there is milk in a gallon container.
(3.8-L)

WHEN YOU **SPEED** DOWN A STEEP HILL ON A **ROLLER COASTER**

YOUR **STOMACH**
AND INTESTINES
MoVE AROUND
A LITTLE.

YOU CAN GET **YOUR FACE 3-D** PRINTED
TO FIT ON A **LEGO MINIFIGURE.**

If you could flatten out all its wrinkles, your brain would be the size of a **pillowcase.**

Feeling **POSITIVE EMOTIONS** can lessen your **PAIN.**

FINGERNAILS GROW FASTER THAN TOENAILS.

31

MEN ONCE USED SPECIAL SOUP SPOONS TO PROTECT THEIR MUSTACHES FROM DRIPS.

PEOPLE USED TO **THINK** THAT IF A **PREGNANT** WOMAN LOOKED AT **UGLY THINGS,** SHE WOULD HAVE AN **UGLY BABY.**

RUNNING FOR 30 MINUTES CAN TEMPORARILY *SHRINK* YOUR HEIGHT.

Scratching an itch can make it itchier.

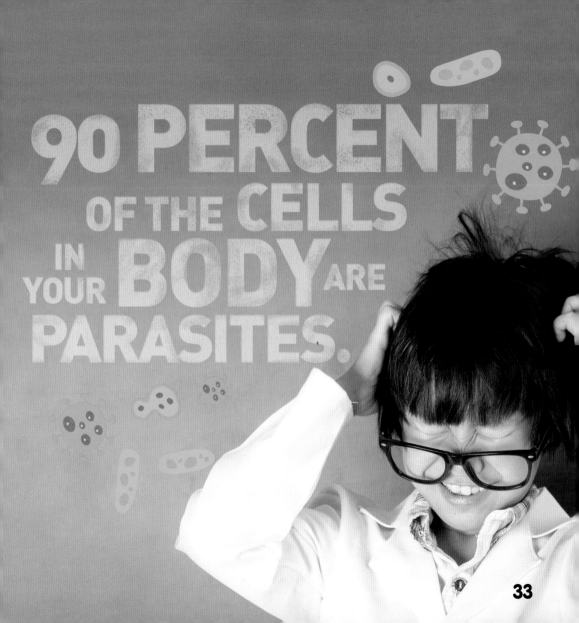

90 PERCENT OF THE CELLS IN YOUR BODY ARE PARASITES.

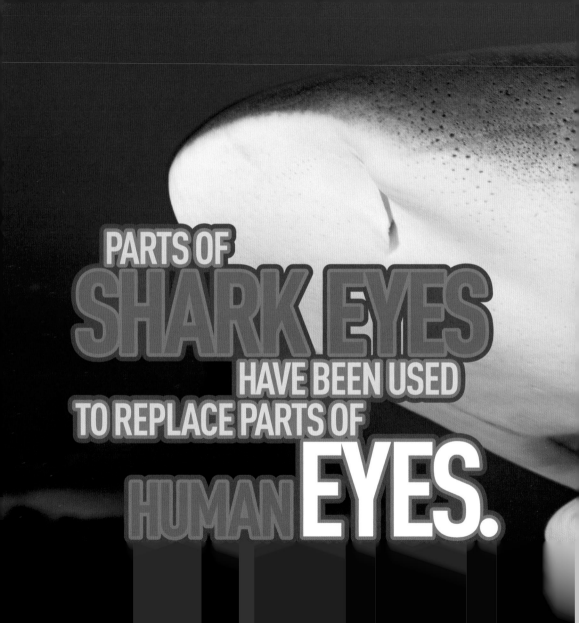

PARTS OF **SHARK EYES** HAVE BEEN USED TO REPLACE PARTS OF **HUMAN EYES.**

If you **chew gum** immediately after **listening to a catchy song,** you are less likely to get the song stuck in your head.

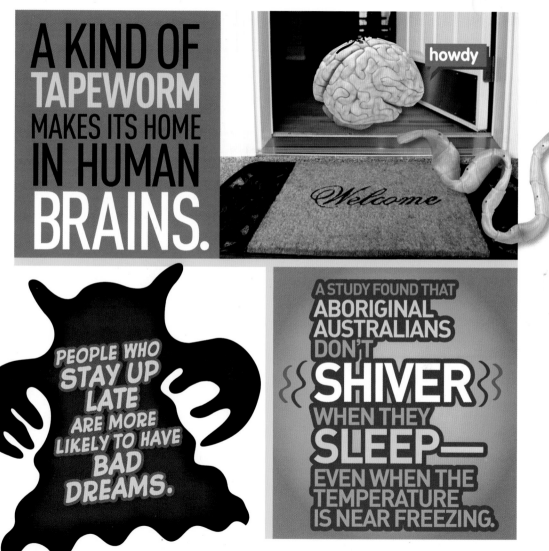

A KIND OF TAPEWORM MAKES ITS HOME IN HUMAN BRAINS.

howdy

Welcome

PEOPLE WHO STAY UP LATE ARE MORE LIKELY TO HAVE BAD DREAMS.

A STUDY FOUND THAT ABORIGINAL AUSTRALIANS DON'T *SHIVER* WHEN THEY SLEEP— EVEN WHEN THE TEMPERATURE IS NEAR FREEZING.

Your heart is powered by electrical impulses.

WOMEN'S HEARTS BEAT ABOUT **EIGHT MORE TIMES EVERY MINUTE** THAN MEN'S HEARTS.

THE HUMAN **HEART** CAN BEAT MORE THAN **THREE BILLION** TIMES IN A LIFETIME.

A RUSSIAN HEALTH AGENCY ADVISED YOUNG PEOPLE TO STOP **TAKING SELFIES** BECAUSE THEY SPREAD *HEAD LICE.*

Your voice sounds lower to you than it does to the people around you.

AT U.S. PRESIDENT **ABRAHAM LINCOLN'S** TOMB, IT'S CONSIDERED **GOOD LUCK TO RUB** THE NOSE ON THE LARGE BRONZE SCULPTURE OF HIS HEAD.

Lincoln HAD THE largest feet OF ANY U.S. president.

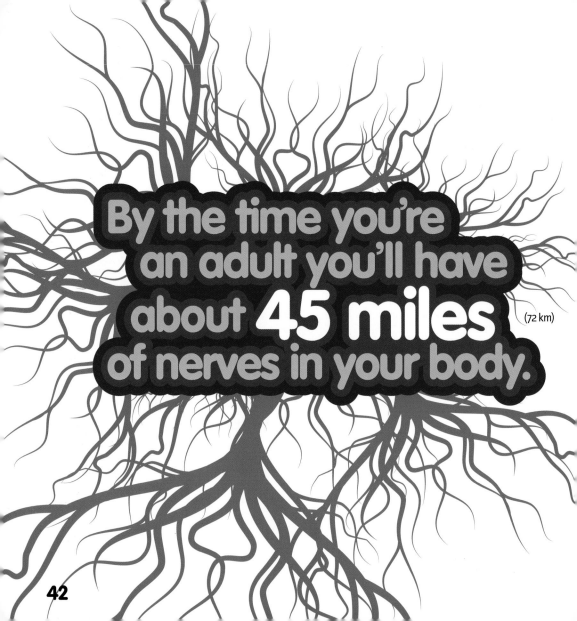

By the time you're an adult you'll have about **45 miles** (72 km) of nerves in your body.

Sounds make  your skull vibrate.

OUR EYES ARE CLOSED FOR ABOUT 10 PERCENT OF THE TIME WE'RE AWAKE.

TINY MITES LAY EGGS ON YOUR FACE.

Some people send text messages while they're sleeping. 😴😴😴

A JAPANESE **MAN** RAN **328 FEET** ON ALL (100 m) FOURS IN LESS THAN **16 SECONDS.**

Nineteenth-century dentists reported seeing patients whose teeth had spontaneously exploded.

Humans have the same number of hairs on their bodies per square inch as gorillas.

45

Your eyes have more than two million moving parts.

YOUR EYE **MUSCLES** MOVE MORE THAN **100,000 TIMES** EVERY DAY.

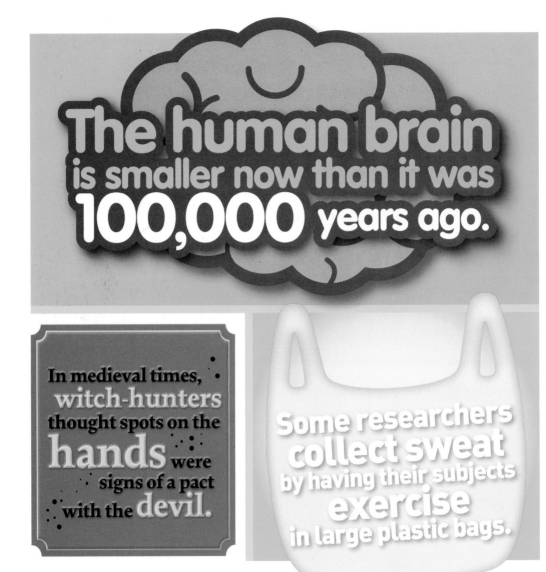

The human brain is smaller now than it was **100,000** years ago.

In medieval times, witch-hunters thought spots on the **hands** were signs of a pact with the **devil.**

Some researchers **collect sweat** by having their subjects **exercise** in large plastic bags.

48

AN AUSTRALIAN MAN **LOST** IN THE HIMALAYA

FOR **43** DAYS

SURVIVED BY EATING **SNOW,** TWO CHOCOLATE BARS, AND A **CATERPILLAR.**

There is a prize for **best musketeer moustache** *at the* World Beard and Moustache Championships.

There are **37.2 trillion cells** in your body.

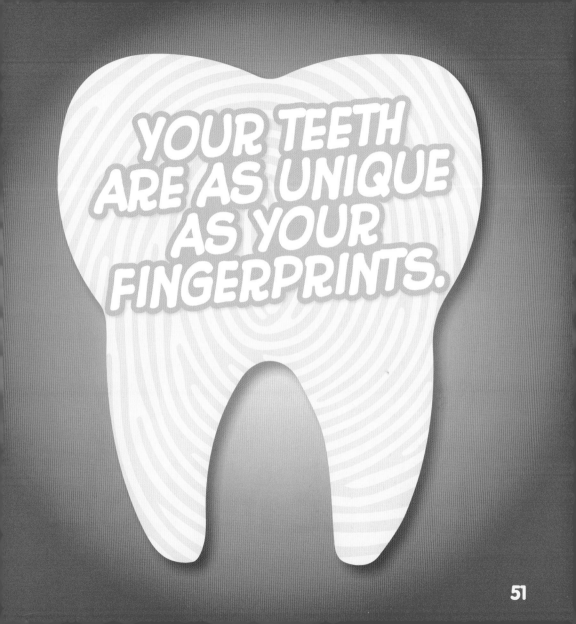

YOUR TEETH ARE AS UNIQUE AS YOUR FINGERPRINTS.

THE WORD "MUSCLE" COMES FROM A LATIN WORD MEANING "LITTLE MOUSE."

A **5,300-YEAR-OLD MUMMY** FOUND IN THE ALPS HAD UNDIGESTED FOOD IN HIS STOMACH.

UVULA = THE SOFT PIECE OF TISSUE HANGING IN THE BACK OF YOUR THROAT

NEWBORNS DON'T HAVE FRECKLES— THEY DEVELOP THEM LATER.

BABIES ARE BORN WITH *BLURRY* VISION.

BABIES DON'T SHIVER.

You have at least

1,000 more
neural connections
in your **brain** than the
number of **stars** in our galaxy.

RESEARCHERS HAVE CREATED A SLEEP MASK THAT MIMICS THE SUNRISE SO THAT IT CAN SLOWLY WAKE YOU UP.

YOU ARE MOSTLY WATER.

BRAIN
75% WATER

HEART
79% WATER

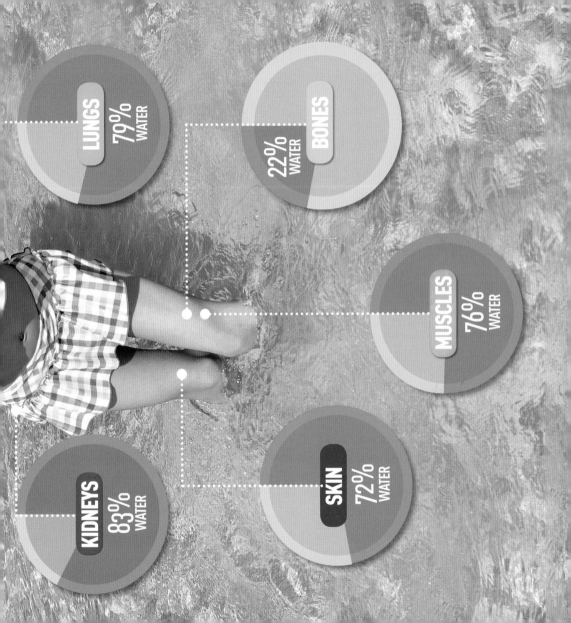

LUNGS
79% WATER

BONES
22% WATER

MUSCLES
76% WATER

KIDNEYS
83% WATER

SKIN
72% WATER

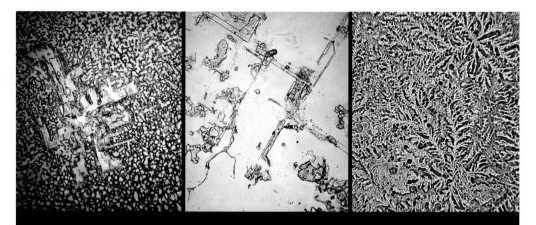

AN ARTIST IN CALIFORNIA, U.S.A., PHOTOGRAPHED MICROSCOPIC STRUCTURES IN MORE THAN A HUNDRED HUMAN TEARS.

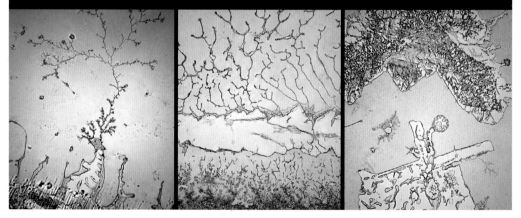

MOST PEOPLE BREATHE THROUGH ONE NOSTRIL AT A TIME.

A British **barber** recently called on the **government** to impose a **"beard tax"** on citizens.

61

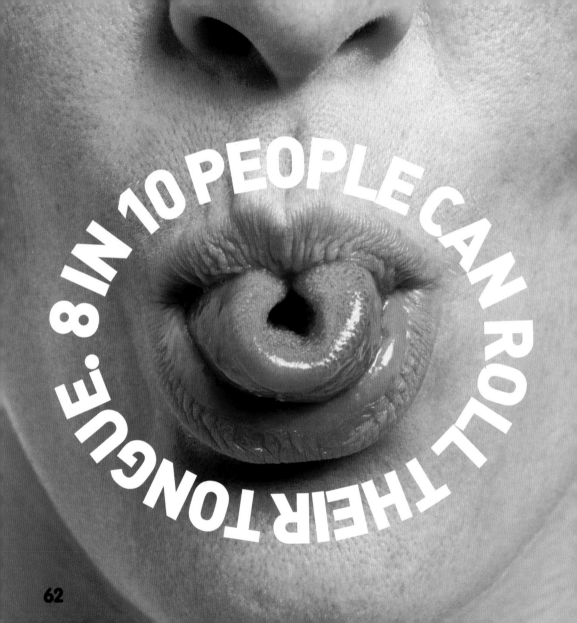

8 IN 10 PEOPLE CAN ROLL THEIR TONGUE.

HUMAN HANDS MAY HAVE EVOLVED SO PEOPLE COULD PUNCH EACH OTHER.

A study found that when **two people in love** sat near each other, **their heartbeats synced up.**

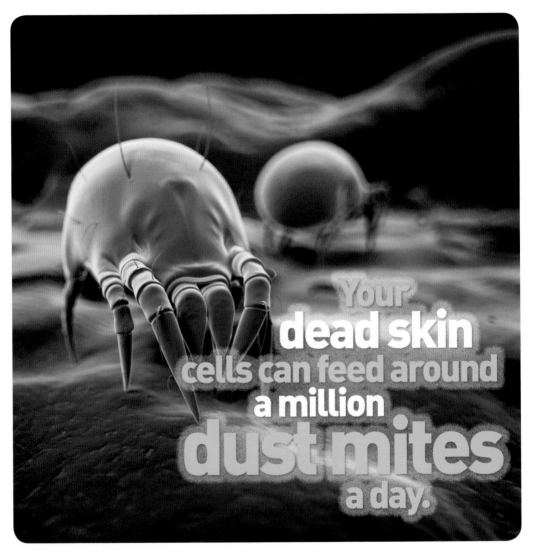

Your **dead skin** cells can feed around **a million dust mites** a day.

You can view **100-year-old** **tissue** specimens at **Australia's** **Museum** of Human Disease.

Some **ancient people** cleaned their **teeth** with a mixture of burned eggshells and the ashes of **ox hooves.**

YOUR **BODY'S** SMALLEST **MUSCLE** IS TINIER THAN A **GRAIN OF RICE.**

1 IN 5 PEOPLE CAN WIGGLE THEIR EARS.

U.S. PRESIDENT **ANDREW JACKSON** LIVED WITH A BULLET LODGED IN **HIS CHEST FOR 39 YEARS.**

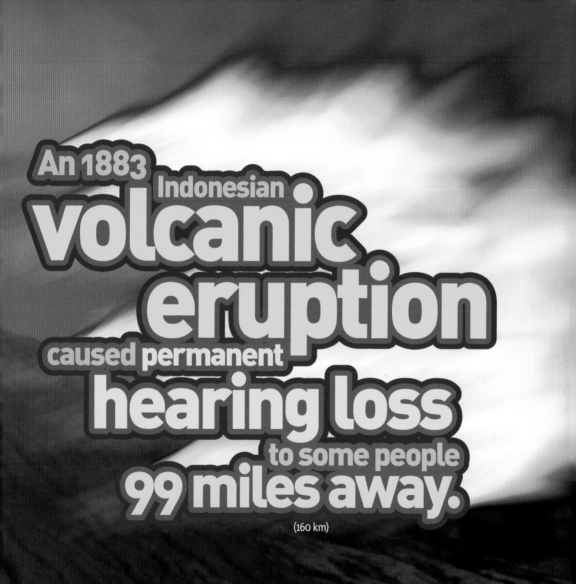

An 1883 Indonesian **volcanic eruption** caused permanent **hearing loss** to some people **99 miles away.**

(160 km)

Your stomach can hold about four cups of chewed food.

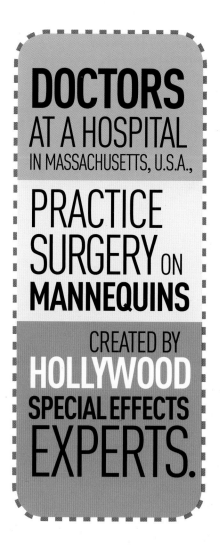

DOCTORS AT A HOSPITAL IN MASSACHUSETTS, U.S.A., PRACTICE SURGERY ON **MANNEQUINS** CREATED BY **HOLLYWOOD SPECIAL EFFECTS** EXPERTS.

A woman once had a two-inch-long (5-cm) leech living in her windpipe.

Asparagusic acid =
the chemical in asparagus that makes some people's pee smell

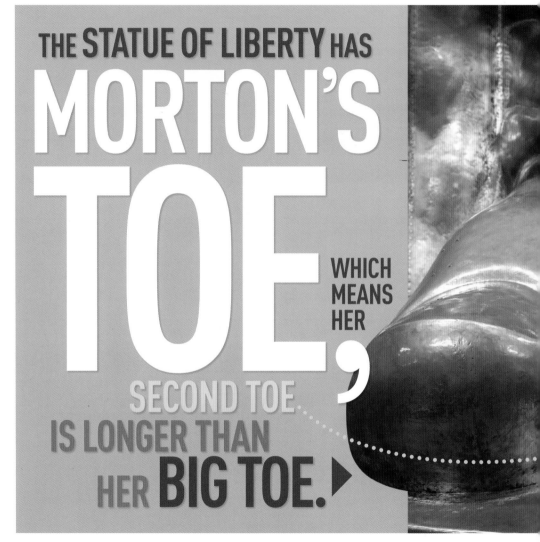

THE **STATUE OF LIBERTY** HAS **MORTON'S TOE**, WHICH MEANS HER SECOND TOE IS LONGER THAN HER **BIG TOE.** ▶

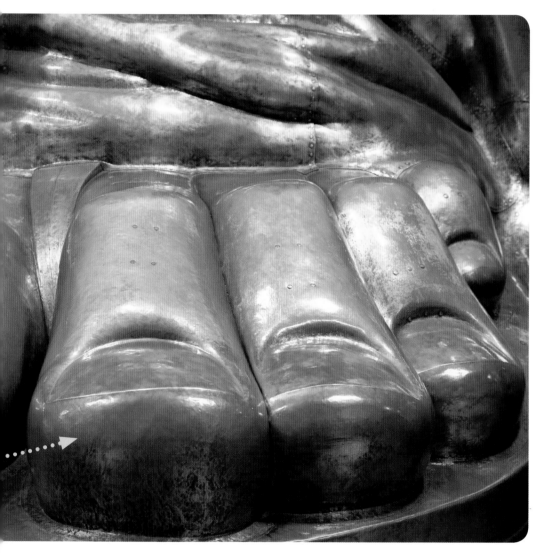

The most finger snaps in one minute: 278

Brain surgery is sometimes performed while the patient is awake.

PEOPLE GET SHORTER AFTER ABOUT AGE 40.

BARBER-SURGEONS = SURGEONS IN MEDIEVAL EUROPE WHO ALSO CUT HAIR

A SPANISH MAN ONCE HELD HIS BREATH UNDERWATER FOR A RECORD-MAKING 24 MINUTES AND 3.45 SECONDS.

A CANADIAN MAKEUP ARTIST RE-CREATED A FAMOUS 19TH-CENTURY PAINTING ON HER LIPS.

A NEW
KIND OF
EARBUD
LETS YOU DECIDE
WHICH SURROUNDING
SOUNDS YOU HEAR—
AND WHICH ONES
YOU DON'T.

A study from **Denmark** found that **kids who walk or cycle to school focus better** than those who travel by car, train, or bus.

YOUR **TONGUE** PUSHES SALIVA DOWN YOUR **THROAT** WHILE YOU'RE **SLEEPING**.

WHEN YOU **BLUSH,** YOUR STOMACH LINING **DOES, TOO.**

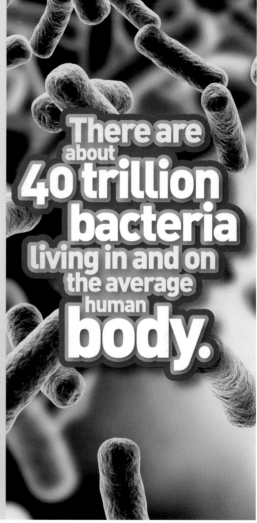

There are about **40 trillion bacteria** living in and on the average human **body.**

RESEARCHERS HAVE INVENTED TINY **ROBOTS** THAT CAN TRAVEL THROUGH **ARTERIES** TO HELP CLEAR **BLOCKAGES.**

YAWNING

ISN'T CONTAGIOUS FOR MOST KIDS

YOUNGER THAN FOUR.

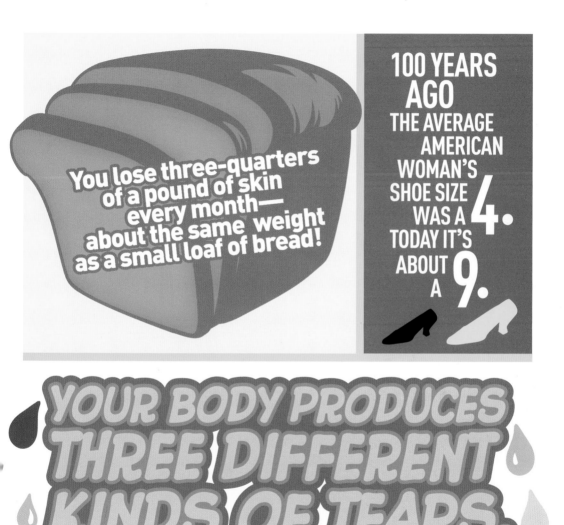

You lose three-quarters of a pound of skin every month—about the same weight as a small loaf of bread!

100 YEARS AGO THE AVERAGE AMERICAN WOMAN'S SHOE SIZE WAS A 4. TODAY IT'S ABOUT A 9.

YOUR BODY PRODUCES THREE DIFFERENT KINDS OF TEARS.

THE world's longest beard,

MEASURING 17.5 FEET, (5.3 m)

IS KEPT IN STORAGE
AT THE SMITHSONIAN
IN WASHINGTON, D.C.

The ancient Maya believed that the first people were made of **mud.**

A COLLEGE STUDENT MADE HIS OWN
3-D-PRINTED
CLEAR BRACES—
WHICH USUALLY COST
THOUSANDS—
FOR LESS THAN **$60.**

SPHINCTER OF ODDI = THE MUSCLE IN YOUR SMALL INTESTINE THAT CONTROLS THE FLOW OF SOME DIGESTIVE JUICES

Your **brain** has about as much memory capacity as the entire Web.

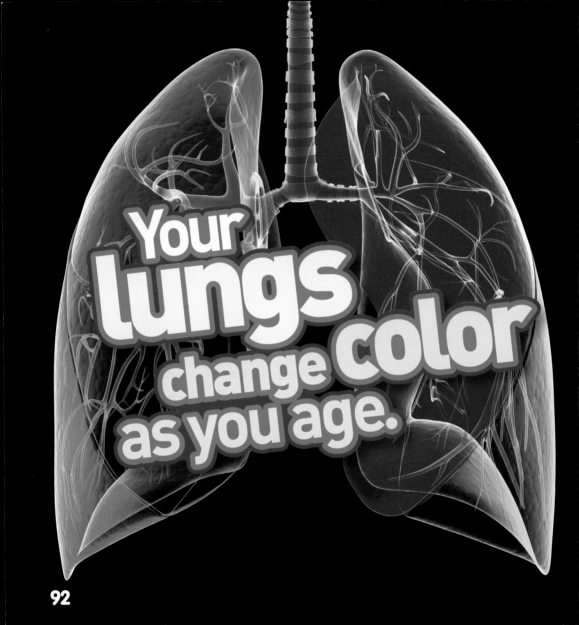

Your **lungs** change **color** as you age.

ACHOO SYNDROME IS UNCONTROLLABLE SNEEZING CAUSED BY BRIGHT SUNLIGHT.

SCIENTISTS CREATED TINY HUMAN BRAINS ON WHICH TO TEST NEW MEDICINES.

The first male Lego **minifigures** didn't have hair.

Your heart makes enough energy each day to drive a truck 20 miles.
(32 km)

THERE IS AN EAR-

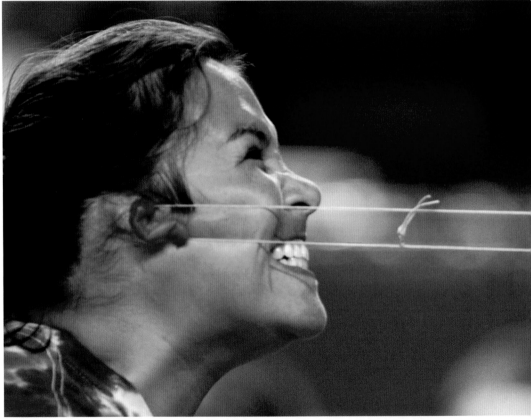

AT THE WORLD ESKIMO-

PULLING COMPETITION

INDIAN OLYMPICS.

It took a Turkish man **5 years** and 11.5 days of **rowing, kayaking, hiking,** and **cycling** to circle the **globe.**

YOUR EYE IS ABOUT THE SIZE OF A PING-PONG BALL.

SOME PEOPLE HAVE SALTIER SWEAT THAN OTHERS.

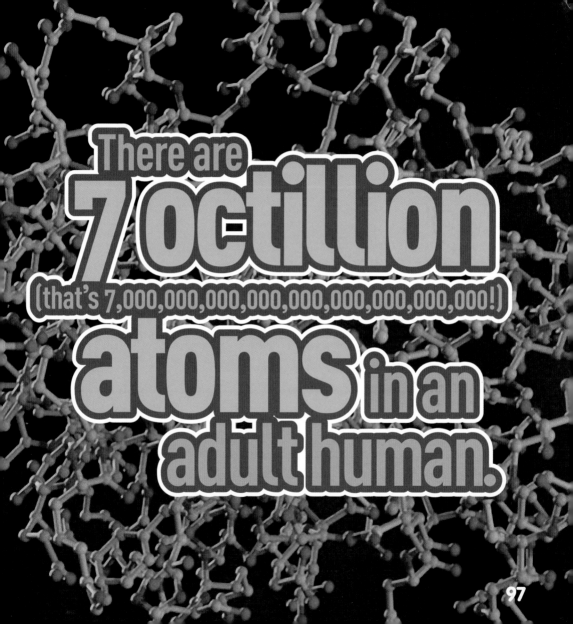

There are
7 octillion
(that's 7,000,000,000,000,000,000,000,000,000!)
atoms in an
adult human.

WHEN UNDER **INTENSE STRESS,** THE HUMAN NERVOUS SYSTEM CAN RELEASE HORMONES THAT GIVE PEOPLE

SUPER
STRENGTH.

A STUDY FOUND THAT **STRAIGHT HAIR** TANGLES EASIER THAN **CURLY HAIR.**

EATING CHEESE MAY PREVENT CAVITIES.

"Snatiation" IS THE MEDICAL TERM FOR **sneezing** CAUSED BY A FULL **stomach.**

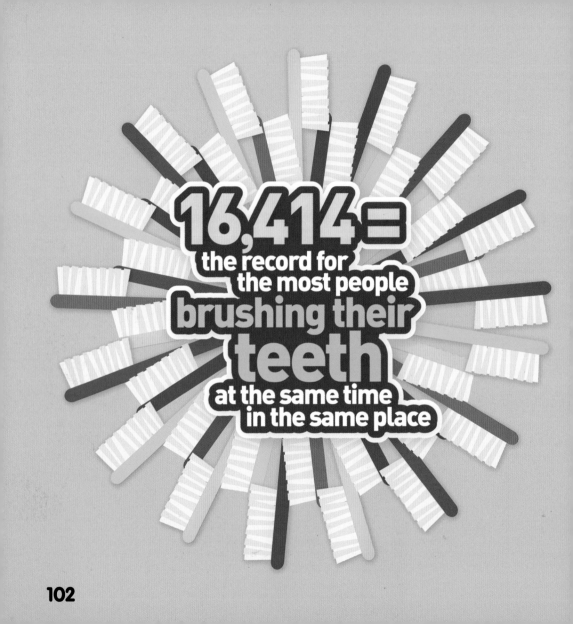

16,414 = the record for the most people **brushing their teeth** at the same time in the same place

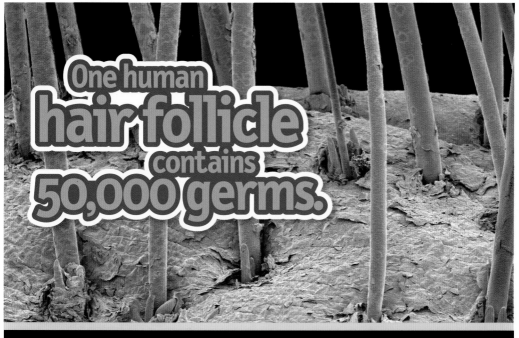

One human hair follicle contains 50,000 germs.

The *bacteria* that caused the *plague* known as the **Black Death** has been around for **5,000 years.**

Scientists say an ostrich's feet are better suited for walking than a human's.

The world's farthest **spit** of a **cherry pit** in competition was **93 feet** (28.51 m) **6.5 inches—** more than half the length of an Olympic-size pool.

During the *Middle Ages, warm goose fat* was dripped into the *ear* to treat *earaches.*

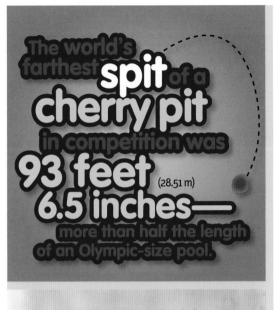

WOMEN IN THE COURT OF LOUIS XVI DREW BLUE VEINS ON THEIR **NECKS AND SHOULDERS** TO SHOW THEY HAD **NOBLE BLOOD.**

IT TAKES **YOU** ABOUT **TWO DAYS** TO FULLY **DIGEST** A MEAL.

It takes a **hummingbird** an hour.

IT TAKES A THREE-TOED SLOTH
MORE THAN A **MONTH.**

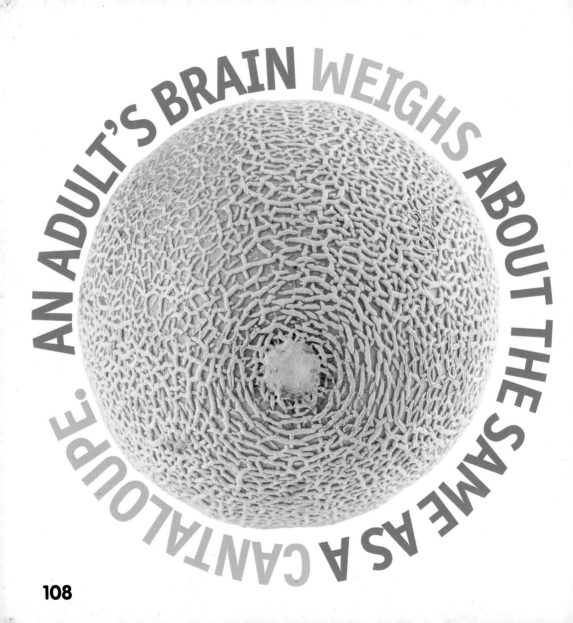

AN ADULT'S BRAIN WEIGHS ABOUT THE SAME AS A CANTALOUPE.

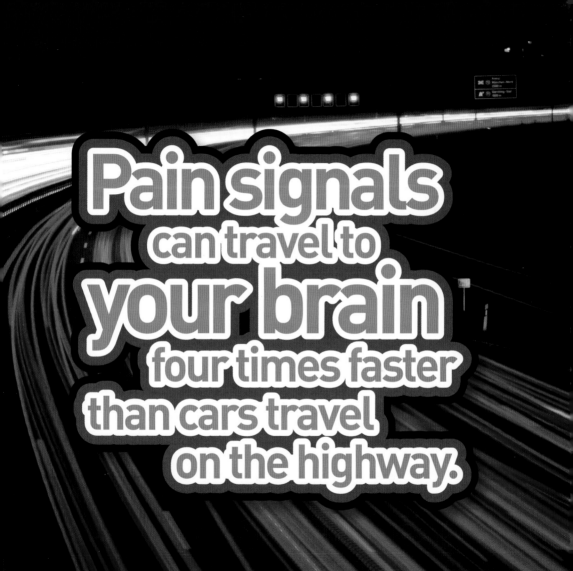

Pain signals can travel to your brain four times faster than cars travel on the highway.

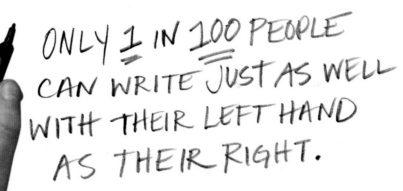

ONLY 1 IN 100 PEOPLE CAN WRITE JUST AS WELL WITH THEIR LEFT HAND AS THEIR RIGHT.

People don't really "crack" their knuckles; the noise you hear is the sound of trapped air bubbles.

A SLEEPWALKER IN LONDON, ENGLAND, WAS FOUND ON THE BEAM OF A 130-FOOT CRANE— (40-m) STILL ASLEEP!

A museum in **Japan** let kids slide into a huge **toilet exhibit** while wearing **poop-shaped hats.**

112

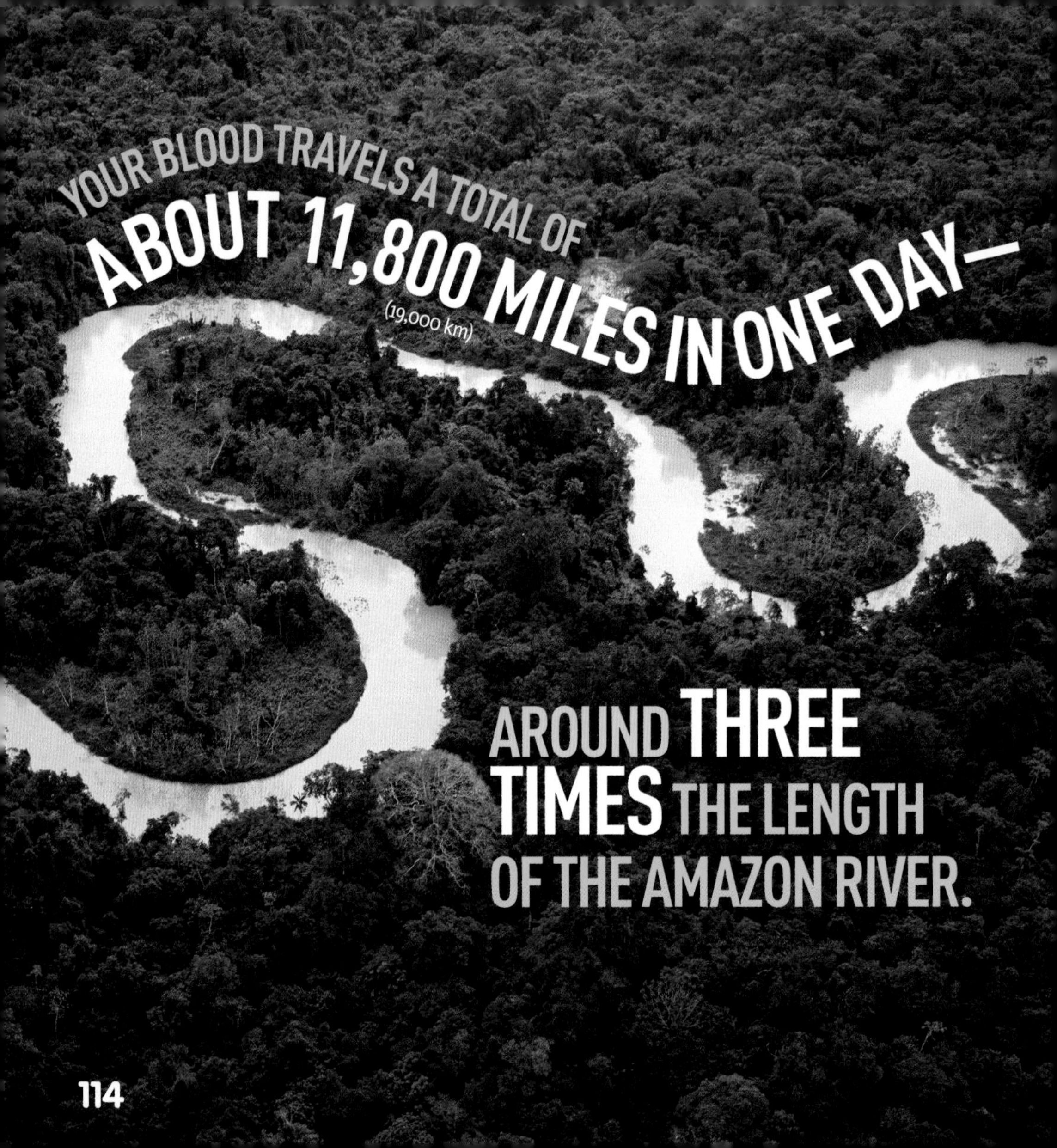

YOUR BLOOD TRAVELS A TOTAL OF ABOUT 11,800 MILES IN ONE DAY—

(19,000 km)

AROUND **THREE TIMES** THE LENGTH OF THE AMAZON RIVER.

Your internal organs can shiver.

In **China,** it is considered taboo to **wash your hair** on the Lunar New Year.

A man set a world record by **covering** his body **in approximately** **637,000 bees.**

Calling the hogs, sawing gourds, and sawing logs = **snoring**

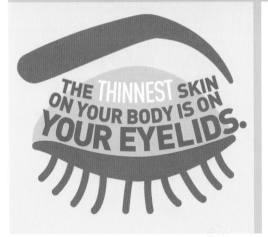
THE THINNEST SKIN ON YOUR BODY IS ON YOUR EYELIDS.

COFFEE CAN KILL THE BACTERIA IN YOUR MOUTH THAT CAUSE BAD BREATH.

DO THESE GLASSES MAKE MY NOSE LOOK BIG?

Ancient **Greeks** used dyed **goat hair** to make fake eyebrows.

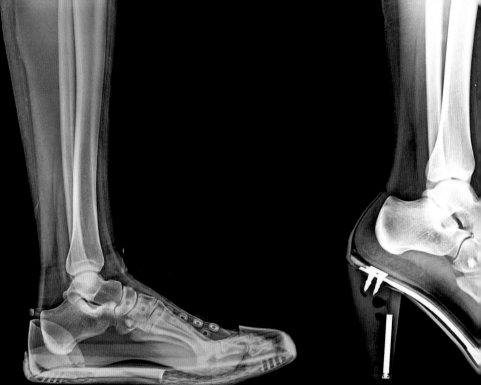

SHOE STORES USED TO TAKE

FEET TO CHECK THE FIT

X-RAYS OF CUSTOMERS'
OF THE FOOTWEAR.

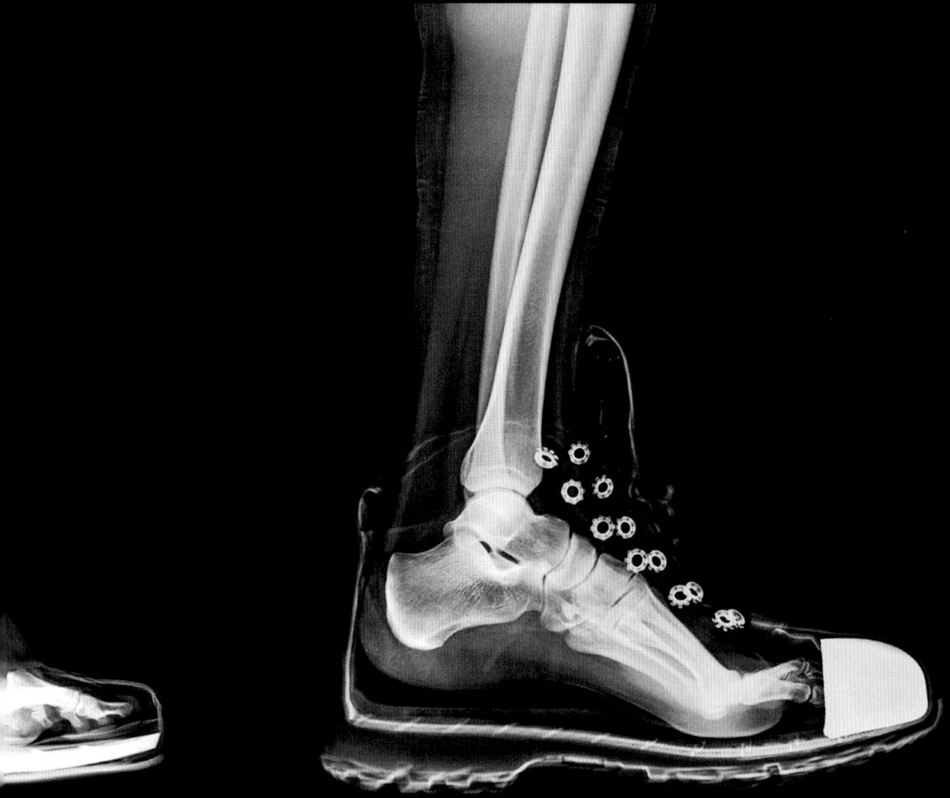

A man whose **SKIN** has exceptional **suction ability** can stick **EIGHT** cans of SODA to his head.

SCIENTISTS ARE WORKING TO CREATE A **WEARABLE FAN** THAT **SPRAYS DEODORANT** WHEN YOU START TO SMELL.

Kids have more **water** in their **bodies** than adults.

THERE'S A VIRTUAL REALITY GAME THAT CAN HELP RELIEVE PAIN FOR BURN VICTIMS.

BEING HAPPY CAN MAKE YOU MORE PRODUCTIVE.

We spend more money when we're hungry.

Putting plain **yogurt** on your skin can help **soothe** a sunburn.

Sometimes the brain favors   one eye over the other.

9 OUT OF 10

PEOPLE HAVE EXPERIENCED

PHANTOM VIBRATION SYNDROME—

THEY THINK THEIR CELL PHONE
IS VIBRATING WHEN IT ISN'T.

STRETCHED OUT, YOUR SMALL INTESTINE WOULD BE ABOUT AS LONG AS A GIRAFFE IS TALL.

YOUR **LARGE INTESTINE** IS ABOUT **FOUR TIMES SHORTER** THAN YOUR **SMALL INTESTINE.**

THE WORLD'S LOUDEST SCREAM

MEASURED **129** DECIBELS—

ABOUT AS LOUD AS A JET TAKING OFF 100 FEET AWAY.

(30.5 m)

You breathe in **more bacteria** released from **tap water** than from your **toilet.**

Your upper eyelid has twice as many lashes as your lower one.

Rubbing garlic on your feet can help fight athlete's foot.

pee-ew!

Every 30 minutes you blink about as many times as there are days in a year.

OUR **SKIN** CAN DETECT DIFFERENCES IN TEMPERATURE AS SMALL AS **1/100** OF A **DEGREE.**

98.76°F

About
**1 out of
every 10
hairs**
on your
head
has
stopped
growing.

RESEARCHERS RECENTLY mapped 97 NEW AREAS OF THE human brain.

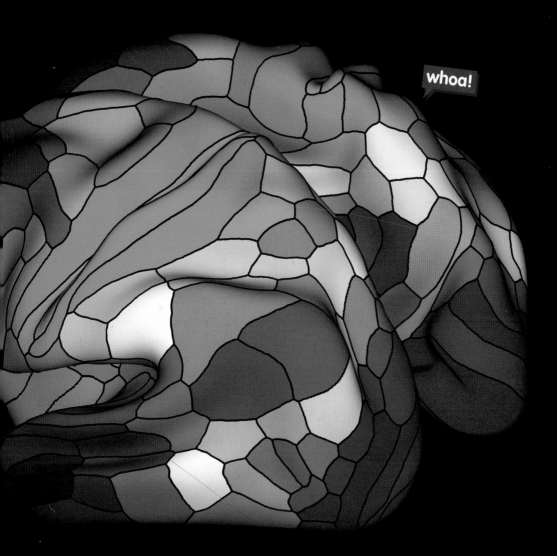

A couple can exchange up to one billion bacteria with a kiss!

11,166 people dressed in red created the world's largest heart shape.

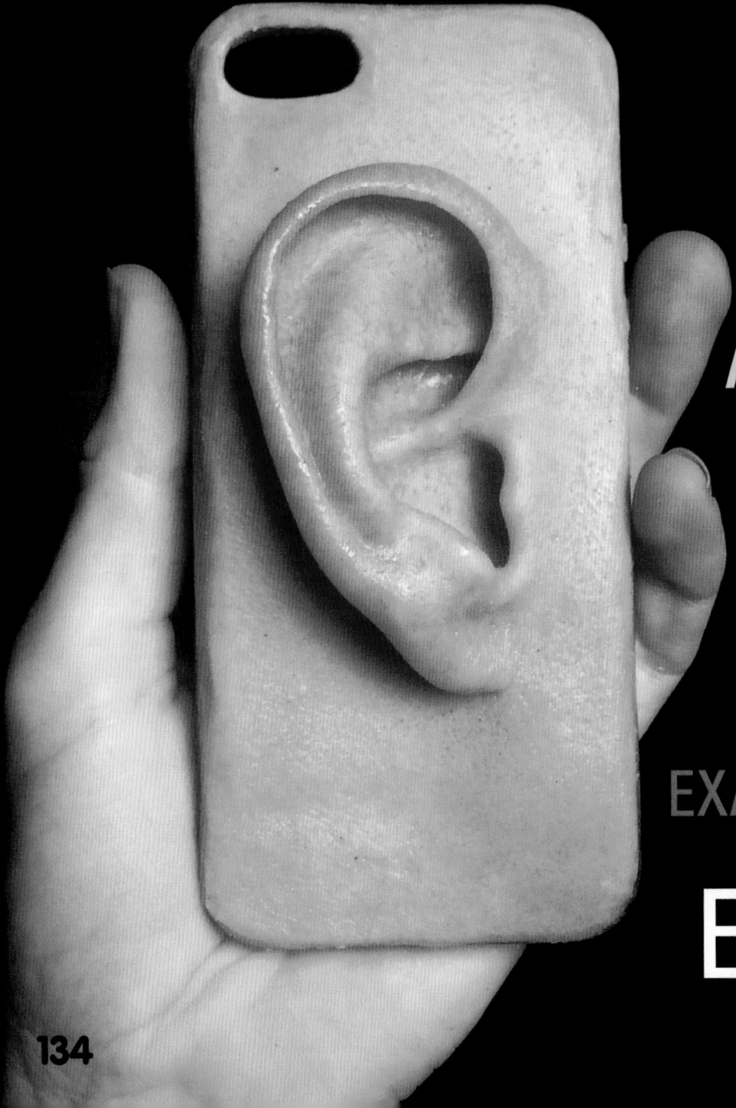

AN **ARTIST** IN LOS ANGELES, CALIFORNIA, MADE A **SMARTPHONE CASE** THAT **LOOKS** EXACTLY LIKE A HUMAN **EAR.**

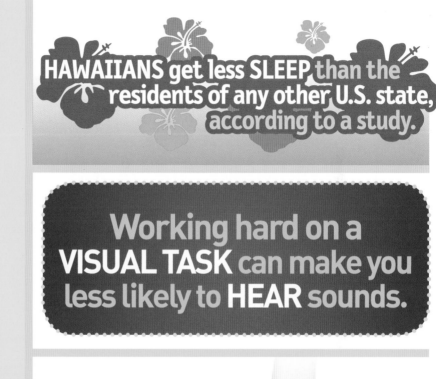

HAWAIIANS get less **SLEEP** than the residents of any other U.S. state, according to a study.

Working hard on a **VISUAL TASK** can make you less likely to **HEAR** sounds.

A study found that **the ankle** is the most satisfying place on the body to **scratch.**

A WOMAN SET A WORLD RECORD BY SIMULTANEOUSLY

9 SPINNING OPEN UMBRELLAS— SEVEN ON HER FEET AND ONE ON EACH HAND.

ANCIENT GREEK PHILOSOPHERS BELIEVED THAT HAVING A GOOD BALANCE OF THE BODY'S FOUR "HUMORS"— PHLEGM, BLOOD, YELLOW BILE, AND BLACK BILE— KEPT SOMEONE HEALTHY.

ULTRAMARATHON
RUNNERS' BRAINS
TEMPORARILY SHRANK
BY 6 PERCENT DURING A
2,796-MILE (4,500-km)
RACE.

Percentage of the general population that is left-handed: 10. Percentage of Major League Baseball players who are left-handed: 25

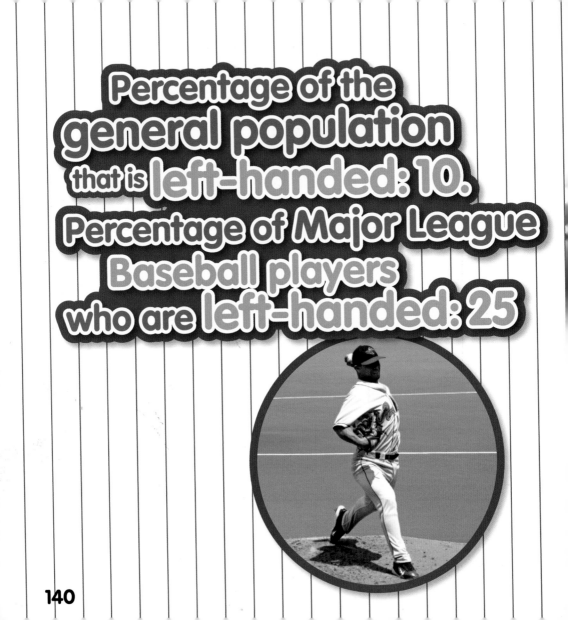

THERE ARE

600 MILLION AIR-FILLED SACS

IN ADULT LUNGS—

MORE THAN ENOUGH TO COVER A TENNIS COURT.

A British field contains a
125-foot (38-m) "fingerprint."

SOME PEOPLE DON'T HAVE FINGER-PRINTS.

The *ancient Chinese* believed that the length of your *earlobe* determined how long you would live.

SURGERY ON THE NOSE IS CALLED RHINOPLASTY.

You can remember something **two times faster** than a **blink of your eye.**

A COCKROACH CAN BITE WITH FIVE TIMES MORE FORCE THAN A HUMAN, RELATIVE TO SIZE.

144

HUMANS ARE THE ONLY ANIMALS WITH CHINS.

IN ANCIENT MESOPOTAMIA PEOPLE THOUGHT A **TOOTH WORM** GAVE PEOPLE TOOTHACHES.

A PRINTOUT OF THE HUMAN GENOME COULD

YOUR BODY MAKES ENOUGH MUCUS EVERY DAY TO FILL FOUR SODA CANS.

KIDS WHO ARE MOVING AROUND DURING MATH AND SPELLING LESSONS **LEARN MORE** THAN THOSE WHO ARE SITTING STILL, A STUDY FOUND.

STRETCH FROM NEW YORK CITY TO LOS ANGELES.

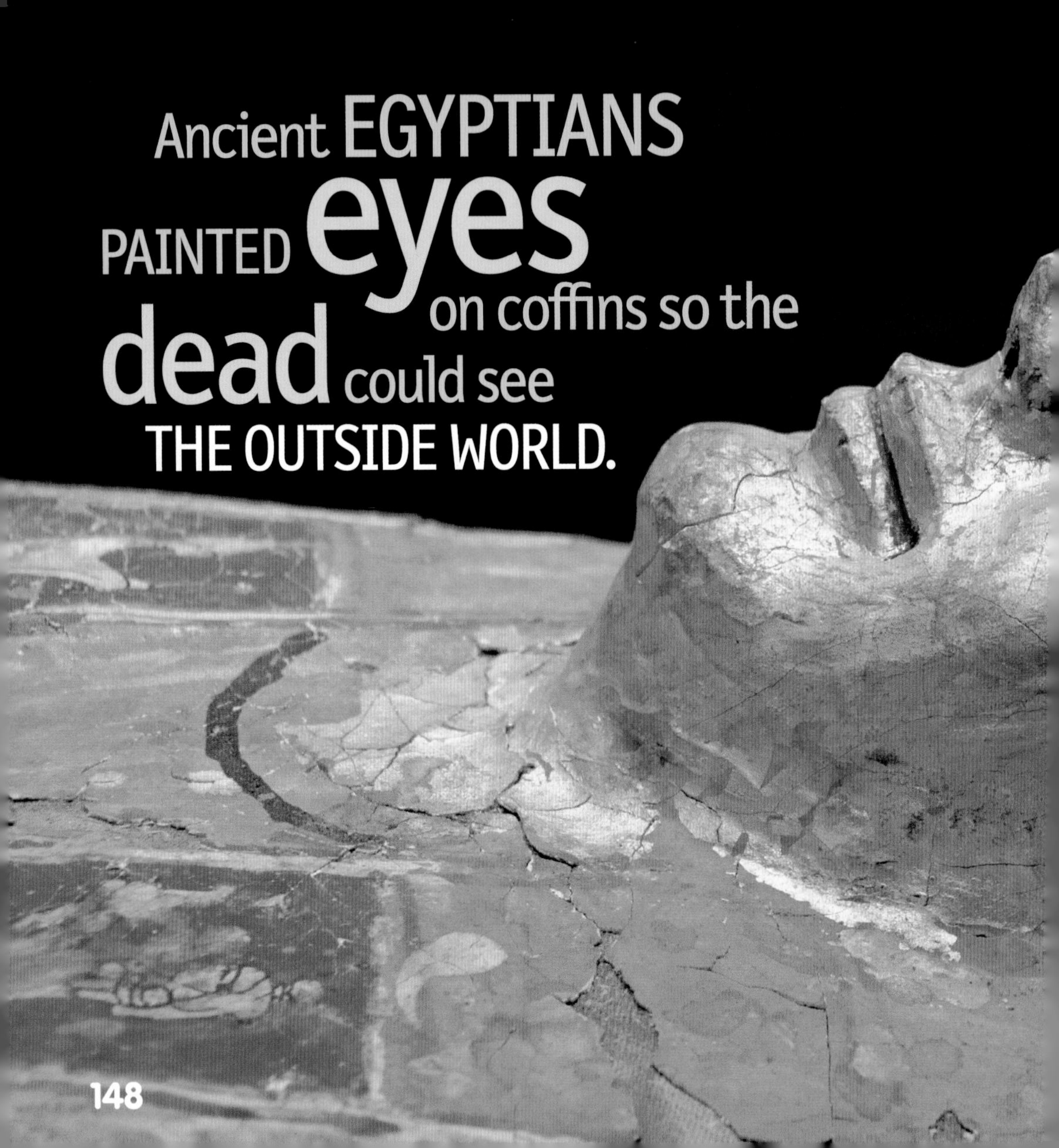

Ancient EGYPTIANS PAINTED eyes on coffins so the dead could see THE OUTSIDE WORLD.

148

149

ZOMBIE FINGER = A FINGER THAT DOES NOT WORK ON A TOUCHSCREEN

The PART on your **BACK** that you CAN'T REACH TO **SCRATCH** with your **HANDS** is CALLED the *acnestis.*

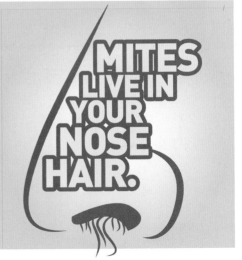

MITES LIVE IN YOUR NOSE HAIR.

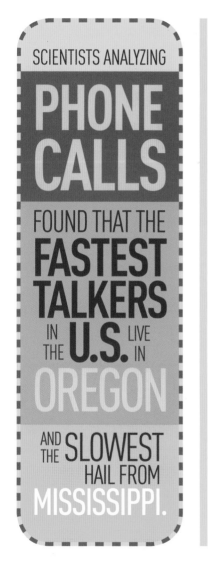

SCIENTISTS ANALYZING

PHONE CALLS

FOUND THAT THE **FASTEST TALKERS** IN THE **U.S.** LIVE IN **OREGON** AND THE **SLOWEST** HAIL FROM **MISSISSIPPI.**

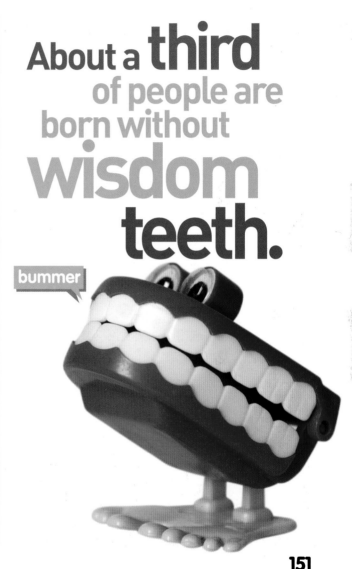

About a **third** of people are born without **wisdom teeth.**

bummer

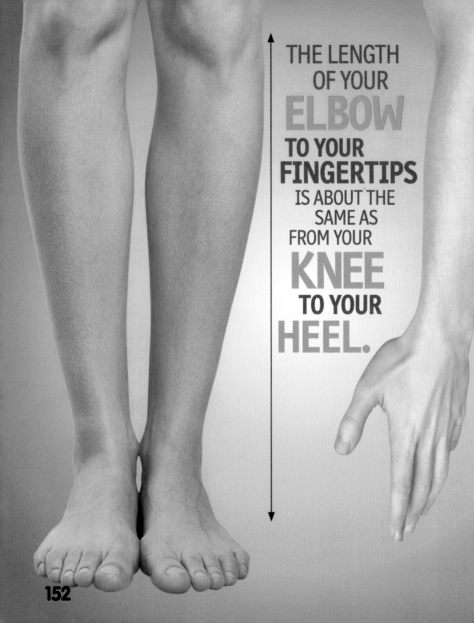

THE LENGTH
OF YOUR
ELBOW
TO YOUR
FINGERTIPS
IS ABOUT THE
SAME AS
FROM YOUR
KNEE
TO YOUR
HEEL.

152

YOUR SENSE OF SMELL IS BETTER DURING HUMID WEATHER.

Newborn **babies** can **recognize songs** they heard when they were in their **mom's belly.**

Most kids younger than two don't get carsick.

LAUGHiNG

CAN HELP
RELIEVE PAIN.

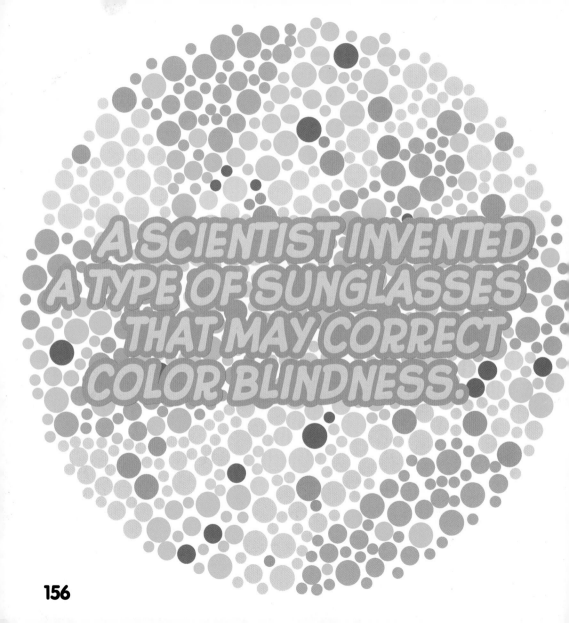

A SCIENTIST INVENTED A TYPE OF SUNGLASSES THAT MAY CORRECT COLOR BLINDNESS.

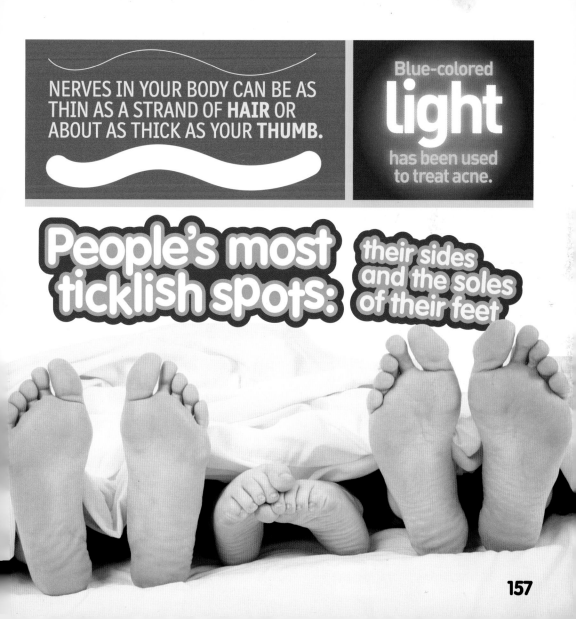

NERVES IN YOUR BODY CAN BE AS THIN AS A STRAND OF **HAIR** OR ABOUT AS THICK AS YOUR **THUMB.**

Blue-colored **light** has been used to treat acne.

People's most ticklish spots: their sides and the soles of their feet

RESEARCHERS HAVE CREATED A WEARABLE

ROBOTIC THIRD ARM

THAT MUSICIANS CAN USE WHEN PLAYING DRUMS.

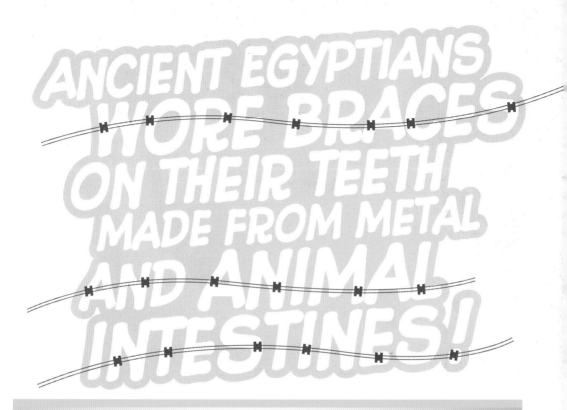

ANCIENT EGYPTIANS WORE BRACES ON THEIR TEETH MADE FROM METAL AND ANIMAL INTESTINES!

A study found that **food tastes sweeter** when you're in a good mood.

THERE'S A **BONE** IN YOUR SPINE NAMED AFTER **ATLAS**, THE MYTHOLOGICAL **GREEK GOD** WHO HOLDS UP THE SKY.

THE WORLD'S LOUDEST APPLE

CRUNCH

MADE BY A HUMAN BITE WAS **NOISIER** THAN A VACUUM CLEANER.

Watching **flashes** of bright light before an airplane trip can help prevent **jet lag.**

THE COLOR OF YOUR EARWAX DEPENDS ON YOUR ETHNICITY.

SWEAT CONTAINS
THE SAME CHEMICALS
FOUND IN PEE.

In **medieval times,** doctors believed some **diseases** were caused by **bad smells.**

MY BAD!

BOYS' HAIR GROWS FASTER THAN GIRLS' HAIR.

SOME PEOPLE DREAM ONLY IN BLACK AND WHITE.

YOU AND A ZEBRAFISH SHARE

85 PERCENT OF THE SAME DNA.

Strands of famous composer **Mozart's hair** were auctioned for **$53,400.**

A study found that a **six-month-old baby** can tell **two monkey faces** apart better than an **adult** can.

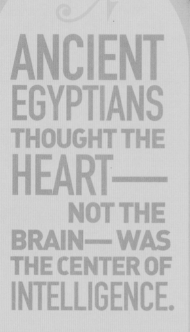

ANCIENT EGYPTIANS THOUGHT THE HEART— NOT THE BRAIN— WAS THE CENTER OF INTELLIGENCE.

THE OLDER YOU ARE, THE LONGER IT TAKES YOUR WOUNDS TO HEAL.

YOUR **LIVER** IS INVOLVED IN MORE THAN **500** BODY FUNCTIONS.

169

YOUR TEETH ARE AS HARD AS A SHARK'S.

chomp!

THE EARLIEST KNOWN

PROSTHESIS
OR REPLACEMENT BODY PART

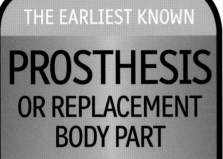

IS A 3,000-YEAR-OLD

WOODEN TOE.

STRESS CAN CHANGE WHAT YOU SMELL LIKE.

A university in England has a toilet that makes electricity from pee.

PERCENTAGE OF THE DAY SPENT SLEEPING:

GIANT ARMADILLO:
75% (18.1 HOURS)

ZZZ...

DOG:
44%
(10.6 HOURS)

HORSE:
12%
(2.9 HOURS)

ADULT HUMAN:
33% **(8 HOURS)**

A dentist in Dubai, United Arab Emirates, **made dentures** using **gold and diamonds** valued at **$152,700.**

A NEW TYPE OF **TABLET** LETS THE **BLIND FEEL** FULL PAGES OF IMAGES AND TEXT ON A **SCREEN.**

HAIR FOLLICLES PRODUCE TINY AMOUNTS OF **HYDROGEN PEROXIDE,** A CHEMICAL THAT CAN BE USED **TO CLEAN WOUNDS.**

Scientists have created a **vaccine** to help prevent **tooth decay.**

Twins have been born more than two months apart.

THERE ARE ABOUT 650 SWEAT GLANDS ON ONE SQUARE INCH OF SKIN.

(6.5 sq cm)

YOUR **NAILS** GROW SLOWER IN THE WINTER THAN IN THE SUMMER.

Your **blood** makes up almost **8 percent** of your total **body weight.**

Scientists can look at scans of sleeping people's brains to see what they are dreaming about.

YOUR **TONGUE** HAS **EIGHT** DIFFERENT **MUSCLES.**

THE **SURFACE** OF YOUR **SKIN** IS MADE UP OF DEAD CELLS.

A NINETEENTH-CENTURY **GERMAN PHYSICIAN** TOOK A **MILLION ARMPIT** MEASUREMENTS FROM **25,000 PATIENTS** TO DETERMINE HUMAN **BODY TEMPERATURE.**

PUTTING AN **ICE PACK** IN YOUR **ARMPIT** CAN BRING DOWN A **HIGH FEVER.**

"AXILLA" IS THE MEDICAL TERM FOR YOUR **ARMPIT.**

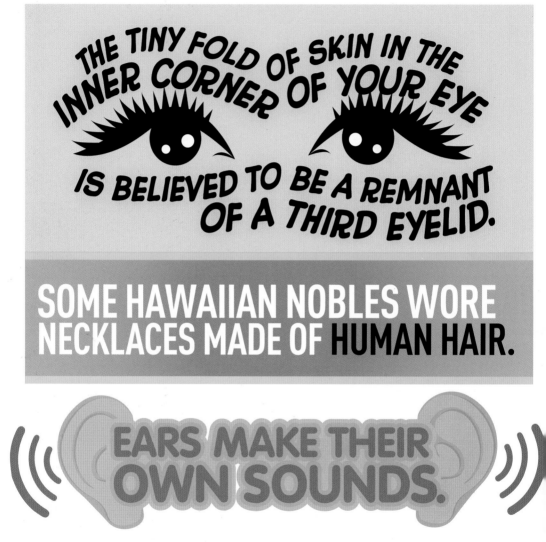

THE TINY FOLD OF SKIN IN THE INNER CORNER OF YOUR EYE IS BELIEVED TO BE A REMNANT OF A THIRD EYELID.

SOME HAWAIIAN NOBLES WORE NECKLACES MADE OF **HUMAN HAIR.**

EARS MAKE THEIR OWN SOUNDS.

The **human heart beats** one-fifth as fast as a **hamster's** and ten times faster than a **blue whale's.**

THE WORLD'S
LARGEST GAME OF
"HEAD, SHOULDERS, KNEES, AND TOES"

WAS PLAYED BY

1,632 PEOPLE
AT ONCE.

The world's **fastest runner** can cover **eight feet in one stride**— (2.45 m) that's almost the length of one and a half bicycles!

RESEARCHERS HAVE CREATED **A WRISTBAND** THAT ANALYZES YOUR SWEAT FOR HEALTH RISKS.

The **bone** that anchors **your tongue** to your neck is shaped like a **horseshoe.**

183

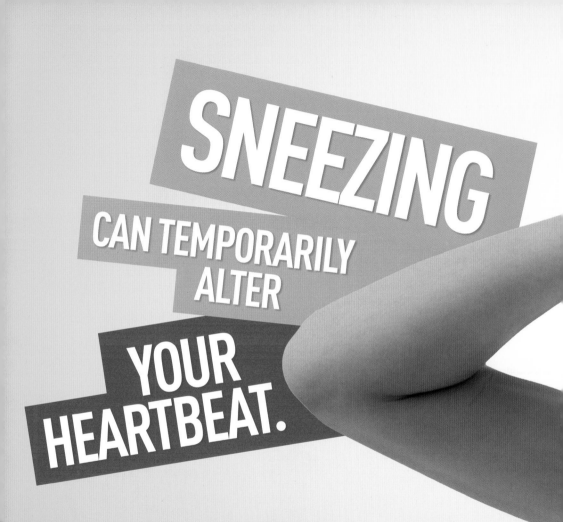

SNEEZING
CAN TEMPORARILY ALTER
YOUR HEARTBEAT.

AN ENGLISH WOMAN ONCE SNEEZED FOR 978 DAYS STRAIGHT

184

SNEEZES CAN BLAST OUT **GERMS** A DISTANCE OF **FIVE FEET** (1.5 m) — ABOUT THE LENGTH OF **TWO SKATEBOARDS.**

AN 11-YEAR-OLD GIRL ONCE WON A **FRECKLE COMPETITION** FOR HAVING 160 FRECKLES PER SQUARE INCH OF SKIN. (6.5 sq cm)

YOUR MIDDLE FINGER'S **NAIL** GROWS FASTER THAN THE ONES ON YOUR THUMB AND PINKIE.

Researchers nicknamed **Homo floresiensis**— a long-extinct 3.3-foot-tall species of human (1-m) —the Hobbit.

THE *SHAPE* OF YOUR **NOSE** AFFECTS THE *SOUND* OF YOUR VOICE.

AND DOESN'T IT LOOK FABULOUS?!

Your **eyelashes** and **nails** are made of the same **substance** that covers a **tortoise's shell.**

ANCIENT
EGYPTIANS
BELIEVED AN
ARTERY CONNECTED
THEIR LEFT
RING FINGER
TO THEIR
HEART.

LUNULA=

the pale half-moon shape
at the base of a fingernail

188

YOUR **FOOT** HAS MORE THAN **100 MUSCLES,** LIGAMENTS, AND TENDONS.

Your **BIG TOE** has only two bones—all the other toes have three.

Costume-makers *for the* **Lord of the Rings** *films wore off some of their* **fingerprints** *creating the characters'* **chainmail armor** *garments.*

NEWBORN BABIES HAVE TINY AMOUNTS OF GOLD IN THEIR HAIR.

SCIENTISTS HAVE CREATED A **BIONIC FINGERTIP** THAT CAN HELP AN AMPUTEE FEEL **SMOOTH** AND **BUMPY SURFACES.**

AS ADULTS, **FIRSTBORN KIDS** ARE USUALLY **TALLER** THAN THEIR SIBLINGS.

YOU HAVE ROUGHLY **4,000** TASTE BUDS **ON YOUR TONGUE.**

ONE OF YOUR KIDNEYS IS ABOUT **THE SIZE OF A CELL PHONE.**

Ancient Celts called **tangled hair** *"elf-locks,"* believing **elves** made hair messy at night.

194

PENICILLIN—MEDICINE USED TO TREAT BACTERIAL INFECTIONS—WAS DISCOVERED ACCIDENTALLY.

During his 340 days in space, astronaut Scott Kelly...

...TRAVELED
143,846,525 MILES
(231,498,542 km)
OVER
5,440 ORBITS
OF THE EARTH.

...RAN ABOUT
648 MILES ON A
(1,043 km)
TREADMILL. THAT'S
ALMOST 25 MARATHONS!

...DRANK ABOUT (731 L)
193 GALLONS OF
PURIFIED URINE
AND SWEAT.

...TEMPORARILY
GREW 1.5 INCHES.

THE HEAT
IN ONE MONTREAL,
CANADA,
BUS SHELTER
TURNS ON ONLY
WHEN PEOPLE
HOLD HANDS.

According to **Japanese** folklore, the **god of thunder** will steal a **child's belly button** if it is showing during a storm.

FACTFINDER

Boldface indicates illustrations.

FACTFINDER

FACTFINDER

Since 1888, the National Geographic Society has funded more than 12,000 research, exploration, and preservation projects around the world. The Society receives funds from National Geographic Partners LLC, funded in part by your purchase. A portion of the proceeds from this book supports this vital work.

For more information, visit natgeo.com/info, call 1-800-647-5463, or write to the following address:
National Geographic Partners
1145 17th Street N.W.
Washington, D.C. 20036-4688 U.S.A.

Visit us online at nationalgeographic.com/books

For librarians and teachers:
ngchildrensbooks.org

More for kids from National Geographic:
kids.nationalgeographic.com

For information about special discounts for bulk purchases, please contact National Geographic Books Special Sales:
specialsales@natgeo.com

For rights or permissions inquiries, please contact National Geographic Books Subsidiary Rights: bookrights@natgeo.com

Design by Rachael Hamm Plett, Moduza Design
Art direction by Kathryn Robbins

Trade paperback ISBN: 978-1-4263-2726-1
Reinforced library binding ISBN:
978-1-4263-2727-8

The publisher would like to thank Jen Agresta for her efficient project management style and expert editing of this book, Hillary Leo of Royal Scruff for her keen photo editing skills, and Julie Beer and Michelle Harris for their research and writing of these truly wild and wacky facts.

Printed in China
16/PPS/1

PHOTO CREDITS

Humans are Hilarious ... AND AMAZING!

Wonder how the human body works? Ready to learn more? Take an amazing inside-out tour, from your brain to your toes, in this ultimate guide.

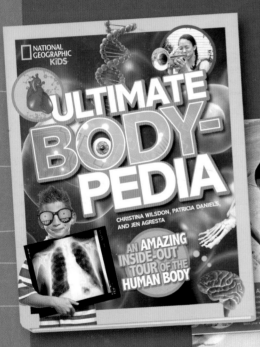